Drained to Numbness

Drained to Numbness

Allyssa Brand-Bey

Brain Waves and Ink

Publishing

Contents

Dedications

To my Family & Friends

Family is near and dear to my heart. There is so much I would not have been able to get through without them. My values, strength, and character were shaped and molded by them. My journey has not been one that was normal at all. My family never let that determine how they loved and cared about me. Even when I scare them, they still show me love and grace. I love them dearly and appreciate them to infinity. Family is the first place we learn about ourselves, having a strong family provides you with a stronger character. To my family, thank you for the support, love, and presence through the years; double thank you to the ones who went above and beyond to support me no matter what. I love y'all.

My circle, y'all have rode these waves with me and never once complained. I cannot thank you enough for the love, grace, respect, care, and understanding you all have shown me. You show up even when the issues are the same. I appreciate the respect, honesty, accountability, love, and care among us all. Without y'all, I would be alone, fighting my heavy battles in silence. We do not talk everyday or see each other all the time, but the bond and love has never wavered. Each tear we have shared, every laugh, and every moment has made us who we are. No matter the situations or the life events that arise, we face them as one. I couldn't have a better circle of friends well, really sisters. We are not sisters by blood, but undoubtedly by choice. Nothing short of family as well! It wouldn't be an accomplishment of mine if I did not recognize my girls. I love y'all and cannot wait for more memories and life!

To my Mother

Behind every strong woman is the strong woman who raised her. My mom was the first example of who and what a woman should be. I thank her more than she knows because I am an exceptional woman. Her love, care, and presence has never wavered. She's walked every battle I've had, just as much as she's walked in my wins. No matter the age, she still walks with me, even when she has no answers, and she is still protecting me.

My mother has shown up for me, even when she had to fight to get there. She never let an excuse remove her from being a part of my life and success. She's shown me what a woman is and who a woman should be. You've done more than you are supposed to as a Mother. Moms are healers, protectors, leaders, supporters, and most of all, the one who shows up through it all. You, Mommy, have done more than you had to, but also did it alone. I'm sure you never imagined my life's storms being hurricanes, but you have fought through them all with me. You never complained nor failed me, even when you couldn't do it all.

I thank you for allowing me to be myself, grow into my own woman, and navigate my many storms the way I needed to. You never question my ability to make it through; you trust my judgment and my strength. You never minimize the pain or dismiss my journey. You cheer with great abundance and love even more.

In the long nights or early days, you remained sane. You handled everything with grace and never cheated the race. I'll never know the silent battles you fought, but what I do know is you never stopped showing up for me. Your presence is loud and uneasy for some, but for me, it is everything. To our village, it's a breath of fresh air to see a mother doing the damn thing.

Mommy, THANK YOU! Thank you for all you have done and all you will do. Thank you for all your dedicated support, the extra work you do and the things you don't have to do. You have never let me go, and for that I am grateful. Thank you for always filling my cup and never letting me fight alone. I love you and will always protect you. Without you, I am nothing, but because of you, I am everything.

Always and forever,

Baby Girl

Introduction

Imagine every illness you have has a consequence you pay. You asked for none of it but were designated to deal with all of it. Penalized for breathing with diagnoses nobody cares for or about.

My life does not have a lesser evil. There is no "this or that", I am left with two bad options and a hard pill to swallow. I don't get a reprieve or a nice break. It's something new after each appointment: a new restriction, new balance, a gadget to buy, and a new compensation to make, but no real fix. Mental taxation with extra exhaustion, not understanding how I got here. It seems like some sick joke. I can't even crack a smile, while all my money goes to health expenses. At 26, I should be living and having fun, but instead, I'm taking care of health things in doctors' offices like it's the club. I'm numb on the inside, and it feels like nothing is really going to change.

Raw emotions, real issues, strains, and stress. Some of these pages document the darkest parts of my life. While others speak to real life scenarios. My story is dark and deep; furthermore it is real and raw. While you read this, you'll take a walk into my shoes and my life: my life as someone who suffers chronic illness, being a black women, and a quick snippet of living in America. But overall, being Human! Many days I wake up to just go through the motions: why me, why all this pain, why these dark walls. We often see those who go through things as strong but never know the pain behind that strength. We as people cannot physically walk in the shoes of others or see them mentally, but sometimes words on paper touch the eyes differently. It's where you can leave the stains of heartache on the page. Many days I cried, morning, noon, and night, asking myself, "Am I really enough?"

Writing is my safe place but also my creative space. I get to bring all of me to the conference room and put words on paper that release the pain and inner me. This book represents a place I never want to visit again but a place many don't have the strength to remain in. "Faking it till I made it" wasn't working anymore; I had to face it to make it. I had to be real with myself and real with my emotions. Suppression began to eat away at my flesh, making me unrecognizable to myself and the world. My battles with depression, anxiety, and PTSD have been a journey within themselves. This book speaks my truth but also my strength. Although it is dark and deep, I hope you enjoy the dive into my life.

Oftentimes people make themselves small but pull out the biggest smile while pouring out the biggest heart. But that is all while hiding an even deeper pain in hopes of relieving the burden from others. We protect the draining measures that could fall onto the ones we love. But truly, is that really healthy? Is it sustainable? We limit who we are and what we feel, to remain acceptable to society. In doing so, we fail ourselves. Nobody lives a perfect life, emotions are very real. We cannot allow the pain to make us feel less than or defeated, nor should we be silenced by the very thing that breaks us inside. Make your pain your biggest enemy and fight it with every breath to protect your compromised breath of silence. Never let your light become featureless because others don't understand or cannot accept your pain. Everyone faces life, but often not the same. We can cross similar obstacles, but we all are equipped differently. Find that therapist, talk in that support group, and look for those pockets of joy in life. Each day, find what makes you happy and complete. Whether we find happiness in a moment of a day or the whole day, pockets of joy keep your heart full and your mind in drive.

Remember to meet yourself where you are but continue to work for your future self. We as humans are taught to stay out the way and never speak of hardship. But why do we have circles and villages? Our circles and villages are pillars of our inner community that hold us up when we are down but also show up no matter what.

Each person is a pillar that represents a safe place, listening ear, celebrator, tear catcher, memorable moments, and accountability. A community is what you make it and how you want to be represented, but also how you want to be seen. Your village can only be as much as you welcome them to be.

You matter just as much as the next person. Reflect on how you show up for people, but also how you protect and love people within your circle and village. Then, ask yourself if you receive that as well. If the answer is no, it is time to reevaluate who you allow in. But also, ask yourself if you even allow them to show up for you in the ways you feel you are missing, and how you show up for them. Remember, people can only do so much; if you keep the door closed, there are only so many ways they can ask you to let them in.

Dark times don't last forever, even if it feels like they do. We become blinded by the pain, sadness, struggle, and loss that we can sometimes miss the wins. Our anger and tears blind us in many ways, which leaves us fighting to find a glimpse of hope and happiness. Losing every ounce of happiness is the worst feeling, but building yourself back up can be even harder. These poems are stories and testaments of my journey. Whether you can relate or not, everyone has a storm they walk. Some may be picture perfect but others are dark and murky, and that doesn't make them null and void. Never discredit someone's storm because it didn't rain in your backyard. This is "Drained to Numbness"... pain with grief on paper.

Drained to Numbness- a feeling of nothing left in your mind, body, and soul. It leaves you in a state of pure exhaustion, pain, confusion, and hurt.

Used in a sentence- life's trials and tribulations left many drained to numbness.

Life

Stories are different, but chapters can have similar threads, bound by different voices. Though highs and lows carry different faces, we as humans connect through situations. Those who are voiceless find peace in these verses spoken for them.

Chasing Peace

No clarity

Extra confusion

Too much noise

Over crowded mind

It's not a place

Or a space

Nor is it a good time

Mind racing

Heart aching

Chest tightening

Survival mode on

Will I ever find peace

Or am I in for the long haul

Allyssa Brand-Bey

Drained to Numbness

Tight chest
Lost of air
Walls closing in
Heart palpitations
With a puddle of tears filling my inner soul
Pain leads to misery
But a broken heart leads to numbness
Empty with nothing left to give
Hurting with no sight of life
Valves pumping hyperventilated air
While your heart waits for the all clear
Machine shocks those fragile wires within
While you listen close
Waiting to hear your happy beat again
Sitting in silence drained to numbness
Wondering if it will ever beat full again

Stress

Everyday is a new day
But stress can face you everyday
Life can be an educator
But it certainly is a test
A test that many face with no equipment
In order to deal we must remove
Take a step away and a breath to recenter
Stress will not stop for a moment
But we certainly can
Alter your thoughts to face stress head on
Stress will break you
But you will have to repair you

Allyssa Brand-Bey

Life

Life has different looks

Life has different walks

But life can be similar

Could be simple and free

Could be complicated and worrisome

Could be encouraging and joyful

Or it could even be dull and blue

Life is simply handed to you

No manual or guidance

Just trial and patients

Happiness

Smile because someone is watching
Laugh because someone is joking
Be carefree like no one is watching
Live like someone is observing
Walk with poise and purpose
But never stop living in happiness
Well because
YOU are watching YOU

Allyssa Brand-Bey

Outside

Small minds kill worthy dreams

Imposed opinions cause re-evaluation

And internal reconsideration

Their failed goals, should be yours

That's why words kill

And support is faint

Faint support because faith fell short

Protect your dreams

Protect yourself

Unsupportive support comes from inside the home

Support Systems

I'm proud of you
That's what they say
Happiness is what they feel
Showing up and showing out is what they do
But most of all they are proud of you
Reach out for helping hands
Theirs reach back
Support systems support your back
Support systems support your tracks
Never will support systems disrespect your back

Present While Absent

Are you here

Or are you seen

Seen to get credit before anything

But did you show them behind the scenes

The never showing up until threats are made

People are here when they need to be

Some like to be seen

While others never second guess

They show up never asked and leave the questions for
the past

But others show their presences when flashes create
proof

Just to say I always show up for you

Broken Promises

I promise I promise
Are the words we hear
But the things we see do not compare
They make promises they can't keep
But expect your promises to run deep
They lack support but want support
Un-requiring themselves to be there
But require you every time
Required to live out your promises
While they walk away from theirs

Growth

We shed our past to prepare

Prepare for the future

It's an ugly process

With a beautiful ending

The challenges we face determine our fate

Will we grow

Or will we sink

Growth makes for better days

But remember growth happens everyday

Safest Place

We can walk through life alone
Or with someone to call our own
They make life fun
Make adventures worth while
But all in all they make days long
Time stops around them
Hours are long without them
Outside is dull when they're without us
They connect the pieces to complete us
Our puzzle pieces
Standing besides us is all we need
Tell your person thank you for giving you the love you
need

Allyssa Brand-Bey

Water the People You Love

Giving flowers never happen

But why

We appreciate that person

So why do we wait until they can no longer see

Or smell the flowers that grow

We water the people we don't know

Why not water the people who help us grow

Water is essential

So is loving the people who help you grow

Watering those you love lift them and lift you

So remember to water the people you love

Dry Eyes

No more water running from my eyes
Everything is dry
At one point all I could do was cry
Cry because I had no say
Cry because life treated me a way
My storm and tears leave me numb
Numb and dull with no resolve
How can I see with my eyes full
I guess that's why now my tears stay at bay

Allyssa Brand-Bey

Dreams

We all dream but do we live our dreams

Dreams are things that never come and go

They stay and wait for us to partake

We live our lives day to day but we never live to play

We work to provide but rarely survive

But when will work be more like play

We have our dreams and visions

But do we get to live them as we see fit

My dreams will be a thing because this journey owes me

everything

Single Home

Mommy you tried
Mommy you won
You did all you could to make me number one
Long nights and sleepless rest
You raised a daughter that doesn't compare to the rest
Doctors and test you struggled to see
Your child fighting every diagnosed disease
From her pain and trauma you made it your own
Wiping your own tears of the fear of unknowns
Decisions you made determined her life
Mommy you chose my best life

Boundaries

Yes is yes
No is no
So why do I need to repeat myself when I said no
Obligations aren't a thing when I say no that's what I
mean
Space is important
Not for you but for me
Access to me can be denied
Your title in my life doesn't grant entitled time
Boundaries I place protect me not you
Your feelings on how I should move
Have nothing to do with what I choose
You may feel your being done wrong
But ask yourself what have I done
Access isn't denied because of truth
It's denied because of YOU

Degree

4,3,2,1
Congratulations you're done
Now the job will come
Your college degree promises that
Or does it
6 months no job but everyone is hiring
Other candidates win but I'm still struggling
Bills become priorities but finances struggle away
And lets not forget scams come into play
Am I worthy
Do I need luck
Or should I just wait
Is it my skin
Or is it my hair
But wait can it be my name
No I know it's my status that changes the game
Do I really not have a job because of who I don't know
Or is it the way of the game

Rejections

Am I good enough or not
Do I deserve a yes or no
Or am I only good enough for no
Do I keep trying
Do I stop
What should I really do
Rejection is never fun
Nor is it comforting
We learn to adapt
Sometimes it's a messages
Or a hidden gem
Other times it's lessons from broken limbs

Judgment

Criticism
Passive thoughts
Rude comments
And no clue what's the real truth
Almost forgetting what's in their dark past
Commenting for reasons they cannot explain
Judging someone else like their past is clean
Remaining humble is always forgotten
Next time you speak of me ask yourself
Who am I to be judging

No Guidance

Someone is trying hard alone
No one at home to guide them along
Breakdowns and let downs is all they know
Because no one cares to help them through
Guidance is not coddling
It's the job you signed up for
Remember nobody asked to be among
All they asked was to be raised
Guide the youth as if they were you

Family

Close but far
There when you need them
Open arms and big hearts
Protection at all cost
Accountability holders
But biggest supporters
Family loves hard
But fights harder
Family ties help major strides
My family rides
And protects my side

Women

I am women

I am staple

World hate

And protection deflection

Created to protect man

But blatantly disrespected by man

No rights

But justification to make the world right

Women are the backbone

Women are the face

A woman deserves all her rights

Toxic

Revolving door

Web of hurt but comfort

Spew of hate

Abundance of disrespect

But toxic feels safe

Breaking the cycle causes growth

Growth causes pain

Growing pains that is

Growing pain is needed

It replaces those toxic traits

Toxic traits that create life mistakes

Distant Love

Personal access can't be granted to all

Distance is what protects our heart

The love is okay but at a certain range

Not everyone deserves your space

Give love when love is given

Forbidden access protects your peace

Your love is precious

Hand it out with chains

A tight hold on it will protect your heart from pain

Black Sheep

Feelings of displacement
Questions of fitting in
Belonging or just placed
Do I really fit in
Feeling different from everyone
Incomplete maybe
Or is it just me
Loved but a stray
Scared of judgment
Will they have anything to say
Or is it fear of being the
Family dismay

Allyssa Brand-Bey

Flowers

Blow in the storm

Bloom in the sun

Grow with gentle water

Break with unexplained pressure

Are we flowers

Or are we human

Broken petals and weakened stems

Will I bloom again

New Storm

Change and growth is a good thing
But pain caused the urge to change
Dark times and murky eyes
The storm is passing
And so is the pain
Here's to the new me
Whew I needed this change
My storm wasn't a choice
But it sure was a test

Allyssa Brand-Bey

Let Down

You pick me up to let me down

You promise me to be around

But when I look up

You've let me down

Stop saying you'll pick me up

Because all you're really doing is letting me down

Trust is broken and lies are flowing

Selfish Ways

Congratulations you picked YOU again
But what about me and my selfless ways
What happened to the team or even the bond we made
You picked you and left me astray
Take care of yourself
Because your selfish ways
Left me drained

Credit

We give credit where it's due

Or were suppose to

Some think they deserve credit

But forget their credit limit is maxed

Why do you need credit for required doings

Deserving credit and having credit

Two different things

Fallen Words

Words fall

Actions sink

But those words still repeat

Please...

Please just don't speak

How about do or

Show the spoken words

Because you sound like a weak beat

Or, maybe just maybe

You are really that carefree

Please act in silence

And collect the fallen beings

Beings of what the words once echoed

They mean nothing to me

Grief

Weird feelings
Racing thoughts
You were just here...
So I thought
Well it felt like yesterday
But years later and I'm...
I'm still grieving you
How do I say I miss you
Without sounding selfish
Or I wish you were here
Growth causes pain
I guess that's why they are "growing pains"
Lost celebrations
Lack of physical presence
And no answers on how you're doing
Grief comes in waves
Chapters and even in spaces
One smell breaks everything
Crippling all around
You closed your chapters
But mine are still being written
...Continued without you
Something I never wanted to do
Achievements and growth claimed while you're away
Looking up to the sky
Hoping you have a front row view

Blur

Misunderstood
Misseen
Misheard
People really miss everything
Sympathy is unimportant
But a listening ear is everything
One moment for a rephrase
A listening quiet ear
Is everything
Not a running mouth
A feeling masker
Not even an invalidator
Or an ear to hear...
With a automated response
For a quick response
Now vocally quiet
Because forcefully silenced
Visible connection is down the drain
Now the speaker has more internal pain

24

A blessing to reach 24
All the fighting and the crying got me here
I guess
From the moment I wake up
To the moment I close my eyes
I'm fighting through my 24
Tired as hell
But stronger than average
My body is tired
And my eyes swollen
My soul tells me keep going
Will I ever be destined to win
Will I ever put my guard down
Living in survival mode drains you
But I guess that's what makes me
24 be graceful to me

Broken System

We seek care
Certified care
Just to be unseen
And even uncared for
Real help is rare
30 minutes in
15 minutes out
Did I receive care
Belittlement and rushed care
Was my chart even read
Is certified care
Even care

Allyssa Brand-Bey

Image Disorder

Images
Mirrors
Social events
It's visuals all around
That perfect image
Well that's hard to see
Let me hide
Wait today I want to be seen
Get my good angle
Wait let me switch sides
Whew... you almost got my bad side
Too big
Too small
Should I post or
Should I ghost
I really just don't fit in here
Let me find my oversized disguise
I hate this feeling
Just so uncomfortable with my outsides
No photo memory please

Sacrifice

Renting out time

Renting out space in your mind

Will I be rented the same

Or am I gambling my time

Making choices and decisions through uncertainty

A choice of yes or no

Should my time be borrowed

Or should I lay low

Blinder

I'm fine
A 4 letter word
Said as a pillar of protection
For inner words and dialogue
Is it a lie
Or just where the words lie
In those pillars
Pain and stillness that wouldn't dare be shared
Shoven words deep down
Protecting the pain of fears
And the ears of those who hear
Those pillars have to stand tall
Protecting all feelings involved

Questions of Walking Away

To stay

Or go

Pack everything

Or unpack everything

Staying is comfortable

But is it respectable

Will you burn bridges

Will you respect yourself

Or will you put yourself in harms way

Ideally you should...

Be smart and walk away

Questions of staying indicates a need to leave

Backbone

Stand up

Be tall

Shoulders back

Chest out

Engage your core

Stop letting them hold your spine

Use your own mind

Control

Weak minds are easy minds

Speaking with assertiveness just to be used

Stay grounded in your thoughts

Bank on your strength

And believe your beliefs

Don't conform to control of others

Allyssa Brand-Bey

Imperfection of Comparison

Beauty standards
Critique of blood
You don't look good
Try looking like him or her
Or maybe reimagine your shape
Too tall
Too round
Too much acne
Too much hair
Just too much for the standard of picture perfect

Projection

Shhh stop talking
Your dreams are too loud
Your aspiration is too strong
Your character too bold
It's disrupting their inner hate
If they can't do it
Neither should you
Their insecurities won't allow
Allow them to be proud
Proud of you nor themselves
How can they support you
When their insecurities envy you

Cover Up

Please lie

Lie to hide my truth

Lie to keep my image unstained

Lie because I want to be safe

Safe from the judgment

Respected for my fake truth

Allow me to be delusional in my brain

And seen outside as a trophy prize

After Thoughts

We thought of you
Well after we did it
We thought of you
Well after we went
We thought of you
Well after we bought it
We thought of you
Well after we ate
We thought of you
Well after we did it first
We thought...
Well after thoughts are never important
You thought of me after the damage
You thought of me after the hurt
You thought of me where I exactly fit
After it mattered and when your image was shattered

Broken Words

Words are stepping stones that crawl out of emotion

Be careful what you say

How you say it

When you say it

Never make someone small

Words can be self projection

Insecurity and lack of self love

Just be careful not to spill damaged views

The Givers of Care

Under appreciated

Under represented

Uniformly disrespected

Never doing enough

But told doing too much

PTO is not included

But mental corruption is income taxed

Never respected

Always expected

Goes unnoticed

Until a hospital stay stamps it

Anger rings out

Distance is imposed

And dissociation is survival mode

Outside crews have a lot to say

But never step in the line of care

And wouldn't dare step in the line of care

Uneven Decisions

Why them
Why the standards
Why someone I never knew
Why scam
Why say no
Why tell me what I know
Why hinder me for what you can't see
Why do you choose what truly hurts me

Space

Home but no room

No space

No invitation

This is yours

But not really

Here's a room

With a few nights stay

While you can stay

Please don't be seen

Occupy the space

But stay tucked away

Go find your own

It's just a temporary stay

Scars and Wounds

Invisible to all

Loud to my soul

Shaped in many sizes

With shackled holds

Unexplainable to the naked eye

Everything to the holders eye

Broken bones hold valid attention

While inner wounds creates unwarranted suspicions

Point of Contact

Always the first on the line
The last to get help
Asked for everything
Helped with nothing
Always waiting for the help to come back
While being asked
Can you help with this
And can you do that
It's never what can I do for you
It's always can you help me

Allyssa Brand-Bey

Battles of the Mind

Pain stops you but chronic pain changes you. There's no days off and no option to be pain free. It's silence with meticulous decisions to carry out your day. No one to lean on, judgement flows, and lack of understanding breaks your inner soul. So many questions with no answer or understanding. Maybe one day it will pay off but for now it's been consecutive years and the storms have yet to let up. Will I sink or will I swim.

Trial and error is the key component to fixing chronic illness. You work daily to achieve good health and freedom. You look for encouragement and answers but never really get anywhere. Your life feels compromised while everyones around you continues on. You hurt watching everyone live and have fun while you silently battle hoping to not impose your feelings onto them. There are many hard truths but also dismissive moments. A continuous journey, its just draining.

Why Me

Pain
Trauma
Needles
Results
This doctor
That doctor
My doctor
New doctor
But why is it me who continues to sit in these seats
I ask myself at least 10 times a day why me
Why do I suffer
Why do I hurt
Why am I in pain
With this kind of pain how can I sleep
Sleep is nonexistent
Standing long is out of the question
Sitting comfortably is far removed
But once again why me
I'll never truly know why me
But my success one day will rewrite the why me

Pain

Everyday someone experiences pain
We ask ourselves
What is happiness
When there's pain
Pain can come and go
But for some it mostly stays
Pain staying takes the real you away
It may feel like it always wins
But truthfully it is watering your wins
Young or old
Seasoned or inexperienced
Pain has no face or age
Just the ability to make you fade away
Day by day and fight by fight
You will beat pain one winning day

Anxiety

Fear

Confusion

Happiness

Sadness

Tremors

Tunnel vision

Medication suppression

Indescribable feelings and never ending battles

Anxiety takes a toll on you

Self criticism and social suppression

Home is safe but also dangerous

It's where overthinking is faced

Never ending cycles confuse you

Will I ever be anxiety free

Allyssa Brand-Bey

What Really Broke Me

Age 7-23 everything pained me
Eager for change but everything broke me
Wanted to stand tall but would fall
Surgery
Diagnosis
And no diagnosis
Tested for so much but little to no answers
Pain while I sleep
Pain while I walk
Pain when I stand
Pain when I'm still
Pain all day everyday
Nobody understands the pain anyway
I owe no explanation when I say pain takes up my day
Fairly young but too young to deal with the hell I pay
I'm over the pain I deal with everyday
But nobody will take my strength away

Procedures

IV

Blood pressure cuff

Confirmation

Operating Room

Fear and racing thoughts

Before the countdown to change

Change that leaves you different

Change that alters you forever

But is the change what your body needs

Recovery and frustration

So you ask

Did my procedure change anything

PTSD

Reminder of trauma

Re-lived pain

Triggers in our mind that only stay

Induced panic

Questions that leave you manic

Healing is a process that can be reversed

One day you're fine

Then next you're crying

You're never exempt

But always finding strength

Pain Lockdown

Unexplainable at times

Damaging to the mind

And harmful to our time

Disrupts our peace

Creates trying times and broken minds

Displayed frustration

And high vaulted anger

Pain is murky

Pain is reversible with growth and therapy

Allyssa Brand-Bey

Numb

Going through the motions

Finding strength to survive

And sanity to thrive

Removed feelings cause a sleeping high

Home is comforting but also triggering

Happiness fades and tears come into play

One by one wiping them away

Each has unexplainable meaning

When will I be whole again

Please remove this numbing cream

It's time for me to be ME again

White Coats

Weight check
Temp check
BP check
Chart update
Now we wait
Sweaty palms and nervous shakes
The white coat isn't too far away
Parking lot prep and inner calming
Fear settles in
What will they say
What do I have
What test will I endure
The trauma I endure
Cannot be explained
All I can say is white coats
Cause me pain I cannot shake

Allyssa Brand-Bey

Twisted Thoughts

Insomnia with toss and turns

Confusion with questions

Frustration with sunken thinking

Am I really normal

Am I really okay

Racing thoughts and worthless feelings

Is this voice in my head really myself

Or is it fear forced

Am I real or am I fake

Do I need help

Or will I just think away

Fear

Fear is funny
But fear is trauma
Fear is blinding
Even mind paralyzing
Crippling thoughts make broken hearts
But is fear really in my heart
Fear damages dreams in a worry way
How can I win with worry on my brain
Will I fear my life away
Or will I win with every dream

Allyssa Brand-Bey

Silent Suffering

Shhh your tears are too loud

Now your pain is even louder

Quiet your problems the world doesn't care

It's better to remain unseen and unheard

Work on everything alone

Don't be a burden on society

Be seen not heard

Is what my mind says

But my down hill spiral says scream

Scream for help and a healing hug

A ear to listen

You want a rescue team

But settle for the tears that mix with the shower water

streams

Needles

Big pinch
Small pinch
Poke here
Poke there
Blood drop there
Bruises here
One small poke here
And a final poke here
Now waiting on needles
For the answer to be clear

Allyssa Brand-Bey

Suppression

Push

Shove

Hide

Repeat that three times

Yes simply

Close your feelings inside

Chin up

Now force the smile

You can just cry inside

Always have your head up outside

It can be down inside

Leave those feelings deep inside

Even with your sanity on the line

Society likes it better with those feelings tucked inside

Shackles of Health

Confinement
Diagnoses
Questions
No answers
Pain
Suffocation
Is this really me
Just deal with it
They say
Honestly you'll never be the same
Is there a key
Or a doctor who really sees me
Unfortunately sweetie there is no key
Not even a doctor to see
But here's a new diagnosis
Without an explicit thing to read
Another chronic illness in the driver seat
Realistically your health runs you
So... good luck breaking free

Allyssa Brand-Bey

Oxygen Leak

Breath in Breat...

Out

Breath in Breat...

Out

The tank says half full

Chest tightness says empty

Some way I'm still afloat

Losing air each second

Do I hold it

Or release it

Quick

Its running thin

Now the cord is punctured

And a slow leak can be deadly

So I'll just hold it all in

Test Dummy

Push

Poke

Pull

Rest

Maybe this test

Or maybe this test

Needles

Blood

And draining test

Are you mentally ready

Because that's the real test

Medication

Take this
Try this
We don't know...
So here's this
It could be this
So here's this
Numbness
Nausea
Blind sight
And who knows the effect
So here's this...
For another test

Four Walls

Let me out
Where do I go
Where's my space
Do I really have a place
Same space
Same view
Trapped with no way out
One space for multiple things
Bags and clutter consume the brain
Can I even walk this way
Grateful for the four walls
But be dying inside to find separate space

Suffocation

Tight chest

Room closing

Space running out

Ideas suppressed

Hard breaths

Not even deep breaths

Rapid inhales and faster exhales

Confinement with anxiety

Racing thoughts

Will I ever make it out

Memories

A quick moment becomes a thought
Placed in storage to reference later
When your presence is gone
A quick file scan brings a rush of tears
Happy or sad remembering all the laughs we had
While you may be gone
Your memory lives on
In storage
In many files
Waiting for me to revisit again

Allyssa Brand-Bey

Gigi

Yellow was your color
So it's mine now too
I get yellow to remember you
You took me under your wing
Making me your mini me
I gave you your name at a young age
When you left me I regretted not seeing you
Angry that I never got to hug you
Gigi I miss you I really do
You held my hand and now my heart
I know you're never too far apart
But now in a birds view
Singing a tune to make room
Room for me to bloom

Papa

You missed me graduate and missed me shine
But I know heaven got you there in time
I needed you here but I needed your sky view
To help me with my blurry earth view
I miss you deeply even though we're on seven years
When you were here you slowly drifted away
That is why purple will always be here to stay
You made life fun and made jokes number one
I just want you to know baby cakes is getting it done

Grandma V

2

2 weeks you were taken away

Now I'm stuck missing you

Wanted to see you

But the clouds needed you

Your sky view is my new view of you

Seeing you from above through my daily view

Adventures and growth you'll guide me through

Clearing my path for success on your end

Even though you aren't here anymore

I'll carry your attitude and strong will

You never deserved this illness but Grandma I'll miss

you

Socially Separated

Depressed

Stressed

Torn

Drained

Far and few expression

Distance and separation

Unintentional judgment

And friendship qualification points deducted

Misunderstanding of internal pain

But expression seems like consistent complaints

Just not feeling the same

But nobody wants to hear pain

Nobody wants to hear the same

Just hide the pain

Going through hell

Doesn't need to be explained

And shouldn't be explained

Allyssa Brand-Bey

The Hidden Struggle

At 24 things made sense

It was never me it was always it

Hiding in the disguise

Or should I say the hyper anxiety

I struggled this whole time

Felt dumb

Inadequate

Less than

Numb

Even unworthy at times

All because my struggle was blind to the naked eye

Daily fights

Questioned intelligence

Wondered mind

Embarrassed at times

But persevered to be

Quite the brilliant mind

Butterfly in the Storm

Years of tears
Unexplainable feelings
Big emotions and little words
Shy but blossoming
Past years broke me
Tearing my wings
Now learning myself all over again
Tattered wings still catching wind
Frustration, confusion, mixed with undetermined
destinations
Tear puddles fill in the holes
Temporarily repairing my tattered wings
Allowing me to brave the storm again
Slowly becoming whole
Weathered storms never washed my tenacity away

Allyssa Brand-Bey

Melanin

The richness of the skin strikes hate from within. This collection dares to speak for the world of Black women navigating life as American women.

Crown

Fro or Straight
Curly or Weave
All natural is a beautiful thing
You can add an inch or two
Adding to beauty
No matter what
A Golden Crown always sits straight
Rejection and threats
Along with outdated beauty standards
Will simply leave no constraints
But if you must or insist
Your jealousy leaves it poised
Beautiful to say the least
While leaving the world annoyed
Your lack of acceptance is null and void
A Golden Crown always shines bright
Please... even with your dull light

Equality

Never enough

Excluded from rights

Questioned on credentials

Treated like nothing

Deemed unworthy

All while surpassing qualifications

Asked to perform everyone's tasks

While being harassed

Brown

Black and brown the most hated around
Looked down on and even preyed upon
Talked about and ranted about
But why does my skin kill them within
Is it jealousy
Is it hate
Or is it fear
Fear of our success
Fear of our growth
Or is it fear they are losing control
Losing control of everything they stole
Or are they just losing control of what they want to
impose

Allyssa Brand-Bey

Black Woman

I am a black woman with the weight of the world on her
shoulders
So beautiful and bright yet so hated but liked
Everyday I fight to be right but the fight is never won
Seen as angry and frightful but never smart and beautiful
With targets on my back and the color of my skin feeling like
a sin
When will I be the one with enough to have
That job
That commercial
Or that talk show
Will I ever be paid my worth or seen as worthy
Being a young black woman isn't easy but it's done with ease
No matter the pain or grief faced
I walk in a path of light and love
Because remaining humble yet ambitious
Will keep me seen for the reasons I was chosen for earth and
everyday life
Being a black girl isn't easy but it is all I want to be
In a world so fearful of me

Women of Shades

Full truth is alway vague
That's just too much to share
Too harsh on the eyes
They say we have to speak in code just to speak black
But never in code about other's gruesome facts
You have to be perfect
Flaws become stereotypes
Screwing the generations after
Overall, our skin suffers from the idea of being too real
We aren't human in their eyes
Our visions aren't their versions
We are just pillars holding up their world

Allyssa Brand-Bey

Generational Confidence

Your fro is too much
Press you hair... you'd look more kept
What are those clothes
Where's the ankle length skirt and button down blouse
Why don't you follow her image
It looks better for the world view
Your weight is too much
Maybe follow her routine
Look the image to win the likes
You're not fitting the white eye
Look kept and be presentable
Long hair
Oiled skin
Covered up
And lips sealed

Black in Appointments

Hello

Based on your chart

Everything looks fine

You just have complaints

Any questions

Good, come back in a year

Have a great day

Now the door is closed

And you didn't hear me speak

Not once did you even ask for name and birth date

So, my healthcare was denied

My questions were unanswered

My mind is in shambles

And my symptoms still progressing

In the four walls of doctor's care

Allyssa Brand-Bey

The Black Bone

Black women...
Black women
I don't think you heard me...
Black women are the go to women
The saving women
The women who have no choice but to defend
But remains defenseless
Scorned
Underrepresented
Torn down in every town
But a hero for every wound
And in every room
Black women are saving grace
While being the most hated face

Standards

Don't be loud
That's classless
Don't celebrate
That's tasteless
Don't succeed
That's unaccepted
Don't be chosen
That's excluding
Don't work hard
That's doing too much
Don't educate
That's showing out
Don't be better
That's excluding
Don't be too Black
That's too much

Allyssa Brand-Bey

Unspoken Red, White, and Blue

They'll never speak the truth, but you'll hear it in the rights of their subliminal and thug like anger trying to push through from a place of inner self-entitlement.

Foundation

Slavery...

Racism

Bigotry

Misogyny

Sexism

Four different words

All the same agenda

America's biggest problem

Allyssa Brand-Bey

World Corruption

Minorities dreams get put on hold
Moved farther away
And harder to obtain
With a moving goal post
Don't get too close
The qualifications will change
Change from fear of equality
Weird when the foundation of America
Is quite literally the backs of slaves
So, how is a goal post moved when
Minorities blueprint is etched in their brains

Bloodshed and Greed

Confusion

Lack of improvement

Hate

Greed

Even dismantling things

Reversal with controversy

Can administration become legal again

Desperation for separation

Poor against wealthy

And no middle ground to be found

Using the backs of millions

The deaths of billions

All to get ahead and walk away with bloodshed

Lack of knowledge because well

DEI hires

Lost in evil can never prevail in civil

Dirty work means dirty hands

Grab the white towel and clean your bloody hands

Go Back

No invitation

Just chains

And seperation

Divison

Treated like threats

But gathered without fear

No reparations

But still paying taxes

Taxes on the chains that brought us

Stereotyped to be evil

Asked to be saviors

While being entertainment for all

Being pushed out by the ones who brought us all

To stolen land and all

Restricted Freedom

On this day freedom rang
But did freedom really ring
Years of control whipped upon us
But today Texas was the last to break free
But I ask again did freedom really ring
Segregation, colorism nation, divided walks
Did freedom really ring
Obama's nation turned into racist hating
Did freedom really ring
Police injustice for unarmed black men
Did freedom really ring
Black women deemed as angry but Karen can get away
Did freedom really ring
White supremacy led by we don't say his name
Did freedom really ring
Black Americans are suppose to walk free
But really we walk with invisible chains
Being black is a job and we still don't get paid
Where are reparations and where is our peace
Where do we matter and where can we thrive
Our success is a threat and our color is a weapon
So I ask again did freedom really ring

Dear Allyssa,

Hey girl, whew it has been a journey! A journey that you never expected, nor did you deserve. Life has chewed you up and spit you out many times, but at a certain point it felt like no end. No matter the encouraging words, you never felt good enough for this world. You just felt like you were made to suffer and hurt. Life has been very unaesthetic and draining, but you never once quit, and that's what matters most. The character, strength, and knowledge you have obtained through the unfortunate situations has made you, YOU.

From age 7-26, all you've grown to know is doctors' offices, new diagnosis, and no time to actually live for yourself. Always under restriction, penny pinching because money goes to medical bills and necessities. Life has been the same thing every day for years: financial hardship, anxiety, depression, self hate, low self-esteem, and never feeling like enough. Even your biggest accomplishments felt small because the hardships prevailed over all.

You've faced things you never really delved into, like facing death as you bleed out in a ER at 13. If you laid your head down that night, you would no longer be. Five surgeries, minimally invasive procedures, endless hours of physical therapy, continued diagnosis, questions of purpose, and the stress of being a burden somehow, you made it through it all with no clue how to. Through hell and high water, you fought even when your body wanted to give up. Anxiety and depression won every time, and you lost important pieces to your puzzle and, most of all, lost yourself to panic attacks and mental dysfunction.

Mental health became crippling in ways you could not explain, but the minute your heart started racing and hands started shaking, you knew to suppress to keep sane. But girl, did that really help? You live in a state of numbness at all times, each day working to pull yourself to safety. You never felt smart but somehow got through. Then, a month after turning 24, the real you came through. ADHD, Lys... the key to the lock that would all make sense. While everything made sense, the world around me never changed. Acceptance was a hard thing for others, but for me it opened my heart to peace. It was never your lack of intelligence, emotions, or understanding; it was the brain connection that failed you. Imagine if 6-year-old Lys had this, life would have been very different. But as you sit here now, a 26- year-old navigating this mental intellectual diagnosis along with anxiety, depression, and PTSD things start to make sense. My school struggle makes sense. I'm learning my triggers, learning myself, but most of all, taking back what I lost for years. I had to mature early to get through, because an underdeveloped mindset would have failed me more. I hate being numb, unhappy, no hope, and no smile. But like my therapist said, sometimes the "fuck it train" is an okay place to be. But sometimes my train feels like it travels the world and I just go too far being numb.

You've advocated and fought for yourself; you found your voice. You made every challenge seem easy but you gained skills through it all. The long nights and earlier mornings, sleepless nights, and long days that continued for years have been altered in your mind. Silent for years, now vocal for days, you no longer allow disrespect; you stop it. Your peace is more important than anyone and anything. No matter the person, you require respect for once protecting voiceless Allyssa. You found your boundaries but also found yourself. You deserve the world, and you now understand that.

Nobody has control over life but you not a doctor, family member, friend, or stranger. Not even financial hardships, which have haunted you most of your life. You hold the keys to every lock in front of you; access is only granted where you see fit. You are humble enough to know your struggle but humble enough to know it never defined you. You have fought and overcome more than you credit yourself for. You may not look like what you've been through, but your internal scars know exactly. Chin up, chest out, head high. You're just getting started with touching the world.

My health challenges

ADHD

Anxiety, Depression, PTSD

Fibromyalgia

PCOS & Endometriosis

Insulin resistance

Hormonal Imbalance

Over 10 orthopedic issues that limit walking, sitting, and driving for long periods of time (also torn hip labrum repair)

5 surgeries and 1 minimally invasive procedure

Acknowledgment

Thank you to everyone who has walked this journey with me and supported me. I appreciate those who took the time to read through, discuss, and help me elevate this piece of art. Without you all, this would still be a thought. When I had my low moments, you all lifted me up and gave me the push I needed. A special thank you to Tia Simone for bringing my poorly deigned cover mock-up to life. Forever grateful and appreciative of all your help.

About the Author

Allyssa Brand-Bey is a new and upcoming author out of Cleveland, OH. She earned two degrees: B.A. in Journalism from Cleveland State University and an M.A. in Communication from Johns Hopkins University. Both helping her define her path in life. As she walks into the author world, she aims to claim her spot and touch lives. Through many storms Allyssa is finding herself and who she is meant to be. Her goal in life is to let people know you have a voice no matter how hard storms roll in.